DEAR SANTA CLAUS

"CHARMING HOLIDAY STORIES FOR BOYS AND GIRLS"

DEAR SANTA CLAUS

"CHARMING HOLIDAY STORIES FOR BOYS AND GIRLS"

VARIOUS

ILLUSTRATED &
PUBLISHED BY
E-KİTAP PROJESİ & CHEAPEST BOOKS

www.cheapestbooks.com

www.facebook.com/EKitapProjesi

Istanbul

ISBN: 978-625-7959-21-6

E-ISBN: 978-605-9285-83-4

Dear Santa Claus

Charming Holiday Stories for Boys and Girls

The Night Before Christmas.

'TWAS the night before Christmas, and all through the house,

Not a creature was stirring, not even a mouse.

The stockings were hung by the chimney with care,

In the hope that St. Nicholas soon would be there.

The children were nestled all snug in their beds,
While visions of sugar-plums danced in their heads.

And mamma in her kerchief, and I in my cap,
Had just settled our brains for a long winter's nap;
When out on the lawn there arose such a clatter,
I sprang from the bed to see what was the matter.

Away to the window I flew like a flash,

Tore open the shutters and threw up the sash.

The moon on the breast of the new-fallen snow
Gave the lustre of midday to objects below—
When what to my wondering eyes should appear
But a miniature sleigh and eight tiny reindeer,
With a little old driver so lively and quick,
I knew in a moment it must be St. Nick.

More rapid than eagles his coursers they came,

And he whistled and shouted and called them by name—

"Now, Dasher! Now, Dancer! Now, Prancer! Now, Vixen!

On, Comet! On, Cupid! On, Dunder and Blixen!

To the top of the porch, to the top of the wall!

Now, dash away! Dash away! Dash away! All!"

As dry leaves before the wild hurricane fly,

When they meet with an obstacle, mount to the sky,

So up to the house-top the coursers they flew

With the sleigh full of toys, and St. Nicholas, too.

And then in a twinkling I heard on the roof
The prancing and pawing of each tiny hoof.
As I drew in my head, and was turning around,
Down the chimney St. Nicholas came with a bound.

He was dressed all in fur from his head to his foot,
And his clothes were all tarnished with ashes and soot;
A bundle of toys he had flung on his back,
And he looked like a pedlar just opening his pack.

His eyes—how they twinkled! His dimples, how merry!
His cheeks were like roses, his nose like a cherry;
His droll little mouth was drawn up in a bow,
And the beard on his chin was as white as the snow.

He spoke not a word, but went straight to his work,
And filled all the stockings—then turned with a jerk,
And laying his finger aside of his nose,
And giving a nod, up the chimney he rose.

He sprang to his sleigh, to his team gave a whistle,
And away they all flew, like the down of a thistle;
But I heard him exclaim ere he drove out of sight,
"Merry Christmas to all, and to all a good-night!"

The Night After Christmas.

'TWAS the night after Christmas, and all through the house

Not a creature was stirring—excepting a mouse.

The stockings were flung in haste over the chair,

For hopes of St. Nicholas were no longer there.

The children were restlessly tossing in bed,
For the pie and the candy were heavy as lead;
While mamma in her kerchief, and I in my gown,
Had just made up our minds that we would not lie down,
When out on the lawn there arose such a clatter,
I sprang from my chair to see what was the matter.
Away to the window I went with a dash,
Flung open the shutter, and threw up the sash.

The moon on the breast of the new-fallen snow,
Gave the lustre of noon-day to objects below,
When what to my long anxious eyes should appear
But a horse and a sleigh, both old-fashioned and queer;

With a little old driver, so solemn and slow,
I knew at a glance it must be Dr. Brough.

I drew in my head, and was turning around,
When upstairs came the Doctor, with scarcely a sound.
He wore a thick overcoat, made long ago,
And the beard on his chin was white with the snow.

He spoke a few words, and went straight to his work;
He felt all the pulses,—then turned with a jerk,
And laying his finger aside of his nose,
With a nod of his head to the chimney he goes:—
"A spoonful of oil, ma'am, if you have it handy;
No nuts and no raisins, no pies and no candy.
These tender young stomachs cannot well digest
All the sweets that they get; toys and books are the best.
But I know my advice will not find many friends,
For the custom of Christmas the other way tends.

The fathers and mothers, and Santa Claus, too,

Are exceedingly blind. Well, a good-night to you!"

And I heard him exclaim, as he drove out of sight:

"These feastings and candies make Doctors' bills right!"

NELLY'S VISIT

ONE summer, Nelly's auntie, who lived in the country, asked her to come and make a good, long visit, and you may be sure Nelly was very glad to go.

She had always lived in the city, and she thought it great fun to feed the hens and chickens and calves, and to watch all the animals and talk to them.

Cousin Fred was about her own age, so it was very pleasant for them to play together. Fred took her around the farm and told her about all the pets, and they soon knew her as well as though she had always lived there.

Milly, one of the horses, would eat out of a spoon, and Nelly and her cousin took turns feeding her. When they went away, she whinnied for them to come back again, but Nelly said, "You shall have some more tomorrow; you mustn't be a piggy-wiggy."

One day Fred and Nelly gathered flowers in the woods, and Nelly made a wreath to put upon her cousin's head.

"It seems just like fairyland out here," she said. "Let's play it is fairyland, and I'm a fairy and you're a brownie."

Fred thought that a very good game indeed, and they played that they lived in the flowers and could change themselves into birds, or squirrels, or people, whenever they wished.

But bye and bye they got hungry, and they couldn't live on the honey from the flowers, as real fairies might; so they spread out the lunch which they had brought and decided to be children again. It seemed as though they had never tasted anything quite so good as that lunch.

One day Speckle, the big hen, made a great fuss because her brood of ducklings went into the water. She flew about here and there on the bank of the stream, and called to them to come back, but the ducklings were having great fun and paid no attention at all to her.

Chanticleer seemed to think they were not very well behaved and needed a good scolding; so he began to strut about and talk at the top of his voice; but the ducklings had their swim and came out as happy as could be.

Nelly thought the little chicks were prettier.

Shep, the dog, could hunt eggs as well as they could, and he always helped them. After he had found a nest, he took each egg carefully in his mouth, and laid it in the basket which the children had brought; and he never broke one.

"I believe he could count them if he tried," said Nelly.

"Of course he can count," said Fred. "When we send him after the cows, he never leaves one behind, nor the sheep either. If one strays away, he hunts for it until he finds it. But he wouldn't hurt one of them for anything, no matter how hard he had to work to bring them in."

They watched the milking, and drank all the warm milk they wanted; and one day they helped churn.

"I believe I could make butter, too," said Nelly.

"Of course you could, dear," said her auntie; "it wouldn't take long for you to learn, either."

Nelly was delighted with this, and wanted to begin right away.

FAIRY STORIES

LAURA, Eva, and Susy are three sisters who are very fond of fairy stories, as most little girls are.

Laura is the oldest, and reads the stories aloud to the others, while Humpty-Dumpty, the kitten, sits near and listen—or, at least, he seems to be listening.

But sometimes he gets tired of sitting still and jumps right up on Laura's book, so she has to stop. Then they all have a great frolic, and very often little brother Harry comes in to join in the fun, and they play until they are tired out.

One story which they like very much is about a little girl who was lost in the woods and wandered about for a long, long time, until she was so tired that she fell asleep on the ground, with the flowers all around her and the birds singing.

But the birds were really fairies and were watching over her to see that she was not harmed, and they sang to her on purpose to lull her to sleep, for they knew how tired she was.

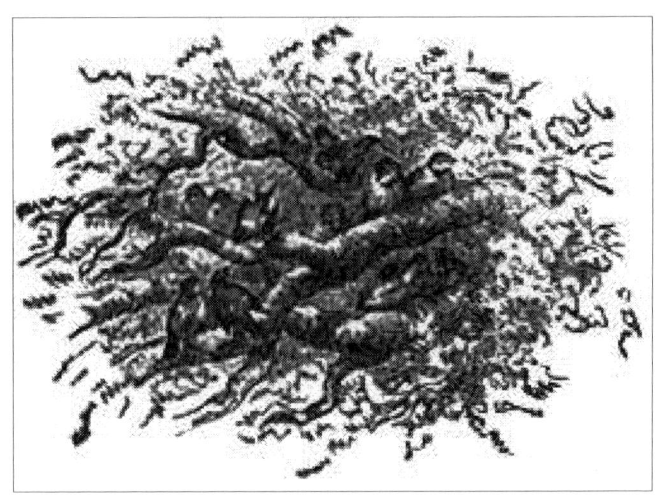

And when she wakened, she understood what they said to her and knew they were fairies, and they led her out of the forest and all the way to her home. They asked her to come and visit them again, too, and promised to take good care of her.

Another of their favorite stories is about the flower fairies who come and dance and sing for little children in the forest when it is very still and the sun is shining brightly.

Laura says she thinks she has almost heard them sometimes, talking to the birds; and they often sit very quiet indeed, with their dollies hugged tightly in their arms, and listen and watch.

Once Eva went to sleep when she was watching like this, out in the grove back of her home, and she dreamed that a fairy came and danced for her and sang the sweetest songs you ever heard.

"She was just like a little girl, too," said Eva. "She was bare-footed and hadn't any hat on her head, and she wanted me to come and dance with her."

"Did you?" asked little Susy, breathlessly.

"Of course!" said Eva. "We danced and danced and had just a lovely time together, and then I had to go and wake up."

"Oh, oh, oh, I wish I could have a dream like that!" cried little Susy; and she went and lay down on the couch right away, to see if she couldn't go to sleep and dream about fairies, too.

But when she wakened, she said that all she could dream about was just a lot of little frogs sitting up very straight on the bank of a brook, with a great, big frog on a great, big log talking to them.

"I think that was a lovely dream," said Laura; and then little Susy was happy.

"Now let's read some more stories," said Eva, and perhaps next time we'll see some really-truly fairies.

—Fannie E. Ostrander.

Kate and Dick had a good many pets. There were Frisk and Ponto and Fuss and another little dog called Fly. There was the pony, Fleet, and the newest pet of all was a dear little colt that Kate's papa had given to her for her very own because the pony she rode really belonged to Dick.

This colt she had named Fairy, and she took great care of it. Fly and Fairy were good friends, and they had a funny way of looking at each other that made the children laugh.

Then the baby that they all loved lived here. Her name was May, and she was Kate's sister. She was a sweet little thing, just beginning to walk and to talk. She could say "chicky" quite plainly, and she liked to toddle out and watch the little girls feed the chickens.

But I can't begin to tell you all the good times the children had that summer. They were happy all the time, and grandma said they were so good that it was really no trouble at all to have them there.

But at last one Saturday evening, papa, who always came out from the city to spend Sunday with them, said they must start for home the next Monday.

They did want to stay longer, but papa laughed and said, "Christmas is coming now, you know, and Santa Claus couldn't bring things way out here as easy as he could get them to you in town."

Then the children began to think of Christmas and to tease grandpa and grandma to come and spend it with them, and of course papa and mamma teased too; so at last they promised, and the children said good-by to their pets and to Kate and May and Dick and went away shouting?

"Good-by, grandma. Now remember you promised!"

After the children reached home they talked of grandma's nearly all the time when they were not talking of Christmas, and Bessie wrote a letter to Santa Claus asking him to be sure and bring a pair of his nicest gold-bowed spectacles for grandma because she had lost her old ones, and not to forget a gold-headed cane for grandpa.

At last Christmas Eve came, and grandma and grandpa were there, and the children hung up their stockings, and Bessie said that grandma and grandpa must be sure and hang up theirs too; then, after they had gone to bed, the smaller children whispered for a long time about Santa Claus and listened to hear his sleigh bells on the roof.

"I don't see how he can get down the chimney," whispered Bessie. "You know he's so fat in all his pictures."

"Maybe he takes off his coat," whispered Clara, "then he wouldn't be quite so big." But she didn't see how he could get down the chimney, either.

Once or twice they were sure they heard him on the roof, and they covered up their heads so he wouldn't think they were peeping, and at last they went to sleep before they knew it.

Willie and Tom were just as anxious as the little girls, and whispered just as much, and they all dreamed of Santa Claus.

Bessie and Clara were the first ones up. They shouted with delight when they looked in their stockings. There was a dear little dolly in each stocking—a dolly with real hair and eyes that opened and shut, and the dollies were dressed very prettily. They were too large to go into the stockings, so they just stood in them, looking as though they were ready to jump down.

Willie found the funniest jumping-jack in his stocking, and Tom pulled a flute out of his. He had everybody awake in no time after that.

Grace was happy when she looked in her stocking. There was a little plush box in it, and in the box was a lovely gold watch; while

Harry found just what he wanted too—a pair of skates.

But grandma and grandpa were surprised when they discovered the spectacles and the cane.

"Who in the world could have told Santa what we wanted most?" said grandma.

Grandpa said he couldn't understand it either, and then Bessie had to tell the secret.

She ran up to each of them and whispered, "I wrote to him myself!"

Then how they kissed her.

All day long the library was kept closed; not a child was allowed to peep in. But what fun they had all day, and what a Christmas dinner, with a plum pudding as big as a pumpkin.

In the evening the library door was opened, and there was the prettiest Christmas tree, all blazing with candles and hung with pretty things; while piled around it were books and toys and everything that everybody wanted most.

And just think of it! There, lying in front of the tree and looking as happy as the children themselves, was a great, big, noble dog, who got up and came to meet them as they trooped in.

"Ooo! Ooo! Ooo!" cried Bessie, bending to pat his head. "What's your name, you great, big darling? Ooo! Ooo! Whose is he, papa?"

"Ask Santa Claus," said papa; and sure enough, Santa Claus stepped out from behind the tree.

"His name is on his collar," said Santa Claus. Then the children all rushed for him for they knew it was grandpa dressed up like Santa Claus.

Afterwards Bessie spelled out the dog's name, "C-a-r-l-o," on his collar, and her own name on a card which was tied to it, and she was the happiest little girl in the world.

But everyone else was happy too, and they all said it was the very merriest Christmas they had ever seen, and Clara and Bessie dreamed that Santa Claus told them he himself had never had so much fun before.

—Fannie E. Ostrander.

OFF ON THE WHEELS

ONE summer Alma and her brother Philip spent their vacation with their auntie, who lived in a beautiful village, so near the pretty country that they could take a ride out into it on their wheels, at any time they wished.

They both rode very well indeed, and they were always finding pretty little spots along the road-side, where they played camp out; for auntie let them take a lunch if they wanted to, and the air was so fresh and pure that they were hungry almost all the time.

One morning they started off quite early with their wheels and their lunch, and they rode out into the country on a pretty road where they had never been before.

It had great trees along the side and a little river winding along with it, and they saw the cattle and horses in the fields, and the hens and chickens and turkeys and geese along the roadside, and once they got off their wheels to talk to a pretty bossy and her calf that were very near the fence.

The bossy was a little afraid they might hurt her baby, so she wasn't quite friendly. But she didn't try to drive them away.

At one side of a farm-house near, a big dog was lying in his kennel, and a great black cat came up to him very slyly and tapped him on the nose with one paw. It was funny to see the dog jump up.

The birds sang, and the hens and chickens talked to each other, and once or twice they stopped to let a flock of geese cross the road in front of them.

Then they came upon a big flock of turkeys, and the gobbler put on airs and pretended he was going to stop them; but they flew past and laughed at him.

By the side of the road in one place, a big, fat, clean-looking pig was standing, sunning himself; but when he saw them, he ran away, squealing.

"You needn't run from us," Philip called after him; "we don't want any pork to-day—we've got chicken for our lunch."

"Yes," said Alma, "and nice, fresh strawberries, and everything good."

They saw a big dog lying near a chicken-coop, with the chickens running over him just as they pleased, and Philip called out again,"Be careful, you little fellows, or you might happen to run down his throat."

They got off their wheels and walked for a little while just for fun; and all at once, as they were passing a barn, Alma cried, "Look! Did you see that cat after the mouse?"

Philip said he didn't; but pretty soon Mrs Pussy came out.

"You didn't get it, did you?" said Alma. "Well, you're fat enough now; you don't need to catch mice."

They stopped to eat their lunch under a clump of trees not very far from a pleasant farm-house. There was a cunning little fat dog lying in front of the house, and as they watched him, up came a bee and lit on his nose.

The little doggy jumped up and barked at the bee; then he sat down and put up his nose in a friendly way, to see what it was.

"Look out, sir!" cried Philip. "You'll get hurt!"

But he spoke just a little too late, for puppy-dog found out his mistake, and the next minute he was running away and yelping at the top of his voice.

"The poor little thing!" said Alma. "Wasn't that too bad?"

"Yes," said Philip, "but he'll get over it pretty quick, and I can't help laughing, it did look so funny."

When they went back to their auntie's, they told her that was the best bicycle ride they had ever had.

—Fannie E. Ostrander.

END

Zeitfracht Medien GmbH
Ferdinand-Jühlke-Straße 7
99095 Erfurt, Deutschland
produktsicherheit@kolibri360.de